Salt and Sand

by Polly Peterson
illustrated by Janet Montecalvo

Harcourt

Orlando   Boston   Dallas   Chicago   San Diego

Visit *The Learning Site!*
www.harcourtschool.com

A beach is a special place. We can
use our five senses to explore it. Let's go!

Use your eyes to look around. You can see the sun. You can see the waves. You are using your sense of sight.

Use your ears to listen. You can hear the sound of the waves. You can hear the sound of the seagulls. You are using your sense of hearing.

Move your hands in the water. The water feels cold. Move your feet in the sand. The sand feels wet. You are using your sense of touch.

Dip your tongue in the water. Do you like the salty flavor? You are using your sense of taste.

Close your eyes. Hold an apple under your nose. Now hold an orange. Can you tell the difference? You are using your sense of smell.

Your senses tell you many things about
the beach. Look up. You can see the blue
sky. You can see the seagulls. You can
see the sun.

Close your eyes. You still know when
the gulls are nearby. You can hear them.

Pick up one seashell from the sand. Does
it feel smooth? Does it feel bumpy? Now
pick up another shell. How does it feel?

Take a walk. The dry sand feels soft and
warm. The wet sand feels hard and cool.

Your senses are working all the time. At the beach there are many things to see and touch at the same time.

Look in the tide pool. Can you see the starfish? How many legs does it have? Can you touch the crab? Hurry before it hides in the sand.

Do you feel hungry? It must be time for
a snack. What would taste good to you?

Some fruit would be great! The peaches smell good. The grapes look juicy. They taste sweet.

The sun is setting. It's time to go home.
What did you see, hear, touch, taste, and
smell at the beach today?